A
FAR CRY FROM
A WHITE APRON

by

Michael & Leslie
Wilson

QUEENSPARK BOOK 39

FOREWORD BY DAME VERA LYNN

D.B.E., LL.D., M.Mus.

WHEN WE REMEMBER the boys who fought in the War, I cannot recall the Bevin Boys ever being mentioned. I think this is a great mistake. We hear nightly about all the other wonderful civilians who played their part, so why not the Bevin Boys, without whom the factories would not have been able to keep going.

I think this story will enlighten many people who have never thought that the Boys played a great part in the war. It is time they were recognised. I hope this story will do this.

Ditchling, November 2000

MICHAEL'S PROLOGUE

I WAS ONLY eight when my eldest brother left home as a Bevin Boy to go coal mining. My memory of this time is very limited but over the last few years I have come to sense the very deep feeling of injustice about his time mining. It is this feeling that prompted me to record his story.

I have read a number of books written by Bevin Boys, but the story that was to emerge from Les was very different to all of these. I can only think that it was being in the very first group that made the difference. This was the start of the learning curve for the scheme and things possibly changed at the next intake. By choosing the colliery he was to work at and not being sent to one with a group of other boys, meant that he was alone. During his time he never came to know of another Bevin Boy selected by ballot in the mine at Llay.

I met Mrs Lewis, his landlady, on a number of occasions. She spoke to me about how she felt, but most of all it was her affection for him and the pride that Les, the first Bevin Boy in North Wales, had lodged with them. She understood the vast divide he had to cross, coming from the south of England to a mining community, and I could tell from what she said that the Lewis family did so much to help.

I have only one real disappointment and that is that my parents are not still alive, so that I could have questioned them about how they felt. The overwhelming feeling I have from talking to others older than myself is that they also were hurt that Les could not go, like his friends, into one of the fighting forces. There seemed to be some sort of shame attached to it all. Maybe they were in some way pressured but that is speculation.

For me, writing his story has been rewarding, for I have come to know a different brother, and appreciate his many attitudes that I had no understanding of whilst I was young.

If any person thinks that coal mining was an easy option, they should check the figures. After many attempts to fill the places of the vast numbers of miners that had left the industry, the wartime government realized that force was the only answer.

ACKNOWLEDGEMENTS

I WOULD LIKE to thank three people in particular, and the many who have listened patiently to my enthusiasm.

First my brother Les, who had to be coerced to get the story from him.

Secondly, Gurminder Bhambra who gave much of her spare time to phrase the questions and extract as much information for me to work from.

Lastly, my wife Kathie, who had to listen, read, advise and correct, and generally put up with me.

Michael J. Wilson

LESLIE'S PROLOGUE

IT HAS ONLY been in the latter part of my life that I have come to realise that ordinary people are as much a part of history as the generals, politicians and the nobility, but they have a great deal less control over their destiny.

We all have a story to tell. Mr and Mrs Lewis did as much for the war effort in time of need as the Field Marshals, but their endeavour in taking me in and happily making me a part of their home life could, as many others before them, have gone unrecorded. There was a common need and even in this small way they played their part.

As a Bevin Boy and the first to go from Brighton, my story is different from that of many other lads sent to work down the coal mines. We were looked on by many as people who wished to evade the war. I was conscripted. I had only one other choice: prison. We were also considered by others as conscientious objectors: many were. They chose to go coal mining as a way of not going into the forces. They were not Bevin Boys but I was classed with them at a time when not to be in favour of the war was abhorrent to many.

This was brought home to me recently on two separate occasions. First, I went to Ovingdean Hall School as part of a request for the fifty year commemoration to mark the end of the Second World War, so that students could question me about my war experiences. It went as follows:

'What sort of a gun did you have?'

'I did not have one.'

'How many Germans did you kill?'

'None.'

'Did you go abroad?'

'Yes, in a strange sort of way.'

'Which country did you go to?'

'Wales.'

'That's not abroad!'

'It was to me.'

'What did you do then?'

'I was a coal miner.'

It ended with 'You weren't in the war.' A view shared by many. Even to the present, we are refused inclusion in the yearly act of remembrance at the Albert Hall or at the Cenotaph march past.

The second occasion I heard of recently from my brother Michael, who had been talking about this period of my life. A friend from St. Andrew's Church, who I have known since 1944, still thought that I had requested coal mining rather than joining the forces because I was a conscientious objector. So the myth survives even to this day, among people I know well.

My view of life and my politics changed during this period. I saw many injustices dispensed to men who were in no position to object because of the need of a job. Even in 1944 life was cheap and the only way to protect oneself was to join a union. I was even forced into this as I was in the coal mines.

I have wondered since, how many Bevin Boys got killed or badly injured whilst mining? Also, how many managed to get out of this because of position and wealth? This happens in all walks of life, so it must have happened in the Bevin Boys' scheme.

The hostile working environment where each and every person is in need of the help and support of the other to get safely through each day, created a solidarity and a comradeship through necessity that filtered into all parts of a miner's life. It was most noticeable when an accident or a strike occurred.

I did not complete my time coal mining until September 13th 1947, so I also saw the change from private to a nationalised industry. We were retained until the other members of the armed forces were demobbed. The reason for this was the state of the country's fuel supplies, coupled with a very hard winter and the need for those that did survive the war to return to the industry.

My lasting memory of this period of my life, is of a group of very ordinary hard working people, willing to accept a young stranger in their midst and help in any way they could to guide and support me.

Many miners that had joined the forces did not return, and were 'buried in some foreign field'. I am still alive. This position could so easily have been reversed. It was a number out of a hat that sealed my fate, for my heart was set on the Royal Navy.

I was told by an old miner from Llay, 'Once a miner, always a miner.' I do feel this now.

Les (Bevin) Wilson.

Les Wilson 1945

A FAR CRY FROM A WHITE APRON

THE FORMATIVE YEARS

I WAS BORN at my grandmother's house, 30 Nesbitt Road, Brighton, the first of my parents' three sons. I spent my young life living on the wonderful new estate at 9 Manton Road, Moulescoomb. We were the first family to live in this house, in this very rural location with cows and sheep entering our vegetable garden on many occasions, much to dad's annoyance.

We were a working class family, with the emphasis on the *working*. Most of my parents' spare time was spent making a better life for us: my dad providing homegrown vegetables, and mum making and mending clothes to help out with the budget. I never did like the knitted bathing costumes she made and even had to suffer the indignity of having my photograph taken wearing one, with my brother Stan .

I went to school in Coombe Road and the friend I had there during my schooldays, I've still got today. We've been mates all these years but the war was to take us in separate directions. I left school the Christmas of 1939, aged fourteen. The war had started a few months earlier.

Jobs were relatively easy to get for lads with a basic education and I started work with my mate on January 1st, 1940, at Zetlands in East Street, as a pastry cook's 'boy'. We didn't celebrate New Year's Day with a day off then, you just went to work.

I only stuck it for two months and then left. I got a better job working for Sainsbury's; a grocery and provisions store at 3 London Road, where I started as a 'boy'. The dress code at this shop was very strict. White shirts with detachable collars were the only types allowed to be worn, the stiff collar was attached with a stud, and the tie was of an appropriate sombre colour. Trousers were always a dark shade. These were my working clothes.

The war seemed very exciting to me so I joined the Air Training Corps for a short period but left and went to St. Andrew's Youth Fellowship. The reason was simple: not God, but girls. As the Fellowship was

Les and Stan,
Brighton
Beach 1930s

connected to the church, my father allowed me to return home after the 10 o'clock deadline he usually insisted upon. He always assured me, 'Nothing good happens after 10 o'clock.' He believed nothing of interest happened after this hour.

In November 1941 I had a very serious illness, peritonitis, and was in hospital for two months. The stay in hospital was extremely expensive, and between the age of fourteen to sixteen I was not insured. So this one serious illness would cripple my parents financially for some years to come. It needed just one ripple on the sea, not a wave, and it was enough to swamp a family of our class. The best insurance policy was a strong caring family structure, which we enjoyed.

When I recovered and was fit enough for work, they moved me from the original Sainsbury's that I had started at to another branch, number 55, at the other end of London Road. I was to work there for the next two years. During that period, I was to experience a lot of things which were to affect my life and the way I would view it in the future.

Sainsbury's was one of the most popular shops along London Road and always packed tight with customers. To suddenly come face to face with a woman who handed me and the lad I was working with a white feather, came as a great shock! It caused quite a scene, as I was just seventeen years old and he, sixteen. Whatever the woman wanted to accomplish, she certainly gathered a hostile audience and was given her marching orders by the manager.

This unfortunate incident affected me badly. I did not think that it was right for youngsters our age to be given white feathers, with the inference that we were cowards. We were as ready as the next man to go into the armed forces when our time came and support our country's struggle, but this unfounded inference was to accompany me for the rest of my life. Even to this day, I am still confronted with it.

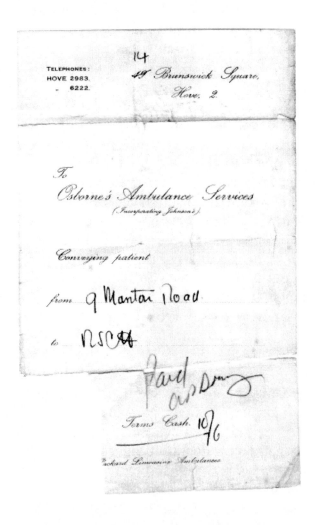

Ambulance bill for taking Les to hospital, 1941

THE CRASH OF A DREAM

The day arrived when I received my call-up papers to join the armed forces. I had a medical in August or September of 1943. It was held in the Odd Fellows Hall in Queens Road, a building that has since been demolished to make way for the Eagle Star building. I passed the medical A1 as did many other people, which is surprising when you think that we were brought up in the days of the depression during the 1920s and 30s, as food was scarce and jobs were almost impossible to come by. People just did not have any money

There were nearly three million people on the dole in those days and there was not the amount of people as are in the country today. My father had lost his left hand at the battle of the Dardenelles in 1915, and so even though he had a job with Allen West, the electrical engineering firm, he was not earning a great wage. Anyway, I passed my medical A1, and my heart was set on going into the Royal Navy.

Then, at the beginning of December 1943, the government had a tombola to decide which of those people who had been called up for military service were to go down the mines instead.

The reason for this new ruling was that Ernest Bevin had allowed many coal miners to leave the pits to go into the armed forces, even though coal was the main source of power in the country. The government had been so keen to build up the fighting services that they had not spared a thought about its effects on the coal mines, and so now there was a shortage of men working down the pits and consequently a shortage of coal.

Everyone who was called up had been given a card with a number on it: this was your call-up number. They put the numbers from 0 to 9 in a hat and decided to draw out two numbers at random. The two numbers drawn were by coincidence, 0 and 9, and anyone whose number ended with these was conscripted into the mines. My number ended in 9 and so I was being sent down the mines. I had no other option than to go to prison. You either went down the mines or went to prison: it was as simple as that. That was what it meant to be a Bevin Boy.

I know that later, people who did not want to fight could opt for the mines, but for me this was not so. All my thoughts of entering the navy were dashed after that ballot. My mate Freddy Evans, had got his choice some months earlier and joined the Royal Navy.

After that first month where two numbers were drawn, only one number was picked out for most of each month's successive call up. Over 20,000 people were drafted into the mines like that. The aim was to ensure a fair system of selection whereby anybody could be enlisted and sent down the mines: rich or poor, lord or peasant.

Looking back, and now having a greater knowledge of how things work and what things were like in England, I have my doubts as to whether all those who were called and fit enough to do this work, did actually go down the mines.

I received my call-up papers on December 24th, 1943. It was not the Christmas present I wanted but it could have been worse, I could have received them on Christmas Day, for there was a delivery of mail on the 25th in those days.

My orders were to report to Haunchwood Colliery near Coventry. The local Brighton paper the *Evening Argus,* interviewed my father, and the report was entered in the paper on the 18th January, 1944. It stated that myself, a grocer and another lad, Laurence Frederick Crump, an artist, were to enter the coal mines - the first to go down from Brighton.

BRIGHTON BOYS FOR MINES

Grocer and Artist

TWO eighteen - years - old Brighton boys left their homes yesterday for Nuneaton, where they are to train for work in the mines under the Minister of Labour's new recruitment scheme.

They were Leslie George Wilson, son of Mr. and Mrs. G. Wilson, of 0 Manton-road, Moulscombe, and Laurence Frederick Crump, son of Mr. and Mrs. F. J. Crump, of 8 St. Peter's-place, Brighton.

Leslie Wilson is well-known as a Server at St. Andrew's Church, Moulscombe, and up till now has been employed by J. Sainsbury, Ltd. His father told an *Evening Argus* representative yesterday: "It's a far cry from a white apron to the black coal mine, but Leslie assures me he will do his best. He had set his heart on Naval service and had actually been passed for it, but it can't be helped."

Laurence Crump, who is a commercial artist, was also looking forward to life in one of the Services as a sequel to his O.T.C. training received at Shoreham Grammar School, and to a year in the Home Guard. He has, however, philosophically accepted the position, realizing that if the powers-that-be think he is best helping the war effort by working in the mines, it is up to him to try his hardest with the job. His father is a well-known dentist.

'It's a Far Cry from a White Apron to the Black Coal Mine...' Courtesy of the Evening Argus.

SEX EDUCATION

In early January 1944, I received a railway warrant to get me to Coventry and was told to meet at the Labour Exchange at a given time.

There was the usual build up of tension as the date of my departure drew near. I was the first of mother's children to leave home and she was obviously worried about my welfare. The fact that it was wartime did not help matters.

On the Sunday evening before I left, I was given my first and only lecture on the facts of life by my father. This was on the insistence of my mother, who wanted her son to be a man of the world. I was taken into the scullery for privacy and the door was firmly shut. My father leant on the wooden draining board and rubbed the stump of his missing hand (it was a lifelong habit of his), then he launched into his well-prepared lecture on the facts of life. I stood before him like a dutiful son and listened:

'Well son, er,...you know, er,... your mum and I have been talking it over.'

Small cough to clear his throat and ease his embarrassment.

'Well as you are leaving home, what I want to say is, well you must know what I am going to say.'

I stayed very silent.

'Well, er.'

This went on for what seemed like a long time with little or no progress at all, until in the end his voice grew firmer, and he said,

'Well son, what I want to say is ....DON'T GO OUT WITH ANY DIRTY WOMEN.'

I could almost hear his sigh of relief. Then the scullery door was opened and my mother looked up from the rag mat she was making and gave me that knowing smile, assured that I could enter the big world with all the knowledge that my father had passed on to me. I was just over eighteen and my sex education was now complete. I have since wondered if he meant that I could go out with any woman as long as she washed!

NEW EXPERIENCES

I duly arrived at the Labour Exchange in Coventry. It was in the main road of the town and near the station so it was not too difficult to find. I arrived there at the stated time and quite suddenly there were about one hundred of us Bevin Boys gathered outside the building. The press was there in full and started to question us, for there had been considerable coverage about our arrival and a lot of hoo-ha about the scheme in general. The government had no idea at the time of the trouble it was going to cause. It was a difficult situation that nearly brought the scheme to a halt. Many people did not think it was right that we should be sent coal mining, which was an industry completely different to anything we had ever known. It was not like going into the army, navy or the air force.

I had worked in Sainsburys most of my life and all of my working clothes were white shirts with stiff collars, so when I arrived at Coventry I was dressed as I would have been when going to work in the usual way. I was now committed to a completely alien job. I felt sure that I would be kitted out with protective clothing sometime in the near future, ready for the task that lay ahead. After all, all the other services are fully kitted out and distinguishable from the general public.

We were at the Labour Exchange for about two hours and then we were marched down into the town centre where we were put up at the Salvation Army doss-house. It was the old hospital building in Coventry right next door to the new hospital which is there now. I went back a few years ago and the old building has gone. There is a large roundabout where it used to be.

Once we had a roof over our heads we all palled up, and like birds of a feather, people of like minds mix together. It ended up with about eighteen or twenty of us together. We found a room that would accommodate us all and later discovered that it was where the kiddies were born in the old days: we were in the maternity wing of the old hospital.

We were to stay for a month and in that time we took the place over. We were paid fifty shillings (£2.50) a week and out of that we had to pay thirty shillings for digs and five shillings for dinners. In the doss-house we were given dinners on the weekends and during the week we got breakfast and tea when we returned from the mine. But at Haunchwood Colliery we had to buy dinners, which cost us five bob (25p) a week, which didn't leave us much spare cash. There was a great deal of discontentment amongst us about this situation and in the end we threatened to go on strike, and they threatened us with prison. Finally the wages for the haulage lads throughout the whole industry were raised to about sixty shillings a week. We liked to think that it was because we had created merry hell.

It was terrible when you think about it. You would have thought that after all the coverage about this first intake of Bevin Boys, they would have been prepared for us - but no. They seemed to be at a loss as to what to do next, and every decision was made on the spur of the moment. I do hope that more thought was given to the welfare of the fighting force.

A bus picked us up from the doss-house at about 7 o'clock in the morning and as it was wintertime it was still dark in the mornings. Haunchwood Colliery was about half-an-hour's ride away, nearly into Nuneaton. It was a small colliery and they only used half of the pit. It was nothing compared to what I was going to find later on.

REMINISCENCE

It was wartime and times were hard, you could not get anything very easily. Things were difficult for us all, but I had learnt something while I was in the Air Training Corps in 1941, which was to come in very handy now.

We had gone to camp in Arundel and went to Ford Aerodrome, which at the time was flying Bostons and a few fighters. Now all of these kids, (I was fifteen at the time) descended upon the aerodrome canteen, where we had our meals. So of course you can imagine, the canteen staff complained. The sergeant in charge shouted for volunteers, 'you, you and you!' I was one of the 'yous'. The sergeant asked, 'Well, what can you do?' I replied, 'Well I can cut that bacon up and I'll cut your bread up.' The sergeant looked at me as though I was boasting. 'Do you know how?' he asked. 'I should do, this is the work I do at Sainsbury's.' 'Are you sure?' He still sounded dubious but led me to a large side of bacon and while he watched, I cut as I had been taught. I fitted the bacon machine up and started to slice the bacon into rashers. 'Well you certainly know what you're about.' He left me to cut the bacon and then the bread. You did not have cut bread in those days. When he returned he said I was very handy, 'We could do with you in here every day.' I could tell that I was on to a good thing so I let him know that this suited me. As he started to leave he said, 'Remember, you don't eat with the rest, you eat with us, here, out the back.' I found out very early in life that the place to be if you want plenty to eat, is where the food is.

In 1944 the same thing happened when we arrived at the colliery. The cook was a woman of ample proportions and she complained bitterly about the extra numbers. 'Oh I could really do with some help now that we've got these one hundred lads thrust upon us for dinners, as we only have the same amount of staff.' At this, somebody asked for volunteers to go and work in the cookhouse. I made sure I was one of those chosen – my best move ever! For the whole month I hardly did anything else but help in the cookhouse during the morning. Just like the Sergeant before, she also told us, 'You don't eat out there with the others, you eat at the back, here with us.' Looking at her size I thought this just has to be good. On top of that I did not have to pay for dinners. The same thing applied, to live and eat well just be near to the food. The food is the thing that counts.

THE TRAINING PERIOD

The training we received was antiquated, thought up by some civil servant I should not wonder. I expect he had sleepless nights wondering what on earth to give the Bevin Boys to do. We were supposed to be A1 and yet we had physical training. One particular time we did a five-mile run, a few of us caught the bus and waited for the others to return.

We had slide shows to explain about coal mining, but this was fatal for me because once in the dark I was soon fast asleep. It was fine until I started to snore, then of course the lecturer had me turning the slides on, so I had to stay awake.

One of the film companies, Gaumont British, or Movietone News came and filmed us at work. What a joke that was. It was then that I realised that much of the 'News' is set up for the occasion. They did not smother us in make-up, but did put dirt on our faces as though we'd been hard at work down the mine. Then we had to queue up for our lamps to make it more realistic. It was then that I started to wonder just how much of the other news is staged to show you what they want you to see.

During this training period I only went down the mine two or three times. I was always in the cookhouse working. There were two of us lads there, myself and Doug Langdell. Doug was a handy friend who lived in Smethwick in Birmingham so we could go home to his house sometimes. He did come down to Moulescoomb on one occasion but I have lost touch with him now. As it was January and very cold, the lads in our digs would bring home a lump of coal or some wood, so each night

Doug Langdell

we had a fire to keep us warm. Why work digging the stuff and not have any? When I think back at what they provided in the way of clothing and accommodation, I think it was disgusting. I recall that we were issued overalls during training (but these had to be returned), a hat and a pair of boots – that summed it all up. My mother had managed to get hold of an old pair of dress trousers for me with stripes down the side. So I wore these and of course my white shirts with stiff collars to go coal mining. What a motley bunch we must have looked, for the others were in the same boat as myself. They never showed that on the newsreel, I feel sure.

I only saw the artist chap, Laurence Frederick Crump, a couple of times during this period. I was never to know what happened to him after this. I think he or his parents had arranged his accommodation somewhere nearby; it was not so rough as ours. Furthermore, with me in the cookhouse, our paths were never to cross again.

The locals around Coventry treated us very well. I suppose we were celebrities to them. They were aware that we did not have a great deal of money, and were always prepared to buy us a beer when they found out that we were Bevin Boys. They knew we had little idea what life down the mine could be like. The men in the car industry and other big companies were earning good money compared to us and they were never tight. People generally did try to help each other whenever it was possible. This wartime comradeship was mainly due to us all fighting a common cause and it was nationwide. The battle lines were clearly drawn. At one time the Mayoress of Coventry came to the doss-house with a few entertainers, and Doug and I did some entertaining ourselves. We sang, 'If I had my way,' and for this we were given the princely reward of some bacon and eggs, which to us was as good as a gold mine.

Bevin Boys' Cloister Concert

Courtesy of the Coventry Evening Telegraph

On a more serious note, we also got scabies while we were at the hostel, due to the dirty area we lived in. We had no health arrangements locally as this had not occurred to the authorities, and my doctor was down in Moulescoomb. So, undeterred, we went to the local hospital and explained the situation. When they found out that we were Bevin Boys they said that they would fix us up. It seemed that being a Bevin Boy opened many doors. We had to strip off and get into a bath of some coloured solution to cure the problem we were suffering from. Someone came in and scrubbed our backs – not a pretty nurse but a great big fellow. When we returned to the doss-house that was not the end of it. All our bedding needed to be changed. It was quite a task, as we were not the only ones with scabies in the building.

One thing that did surprise me while I was there was the number of cockroaches that infested the place. Even though my family was poor, I had never seen them before. The place that we ate in was swarming with them. When the light was put on they scampered everywhere. I hated them and swore never to eat in that area again. So two chaps from our room would get the breakfast and we would eat it in our bedroom, in bed, what a luxury. The other lads in the building hated this.

There were no washing facilities for our clothes, so I would go into Sainsbury's and get some brown paper and send my bits and pieces home to mum, and she returned them washed and ironed. What mums do for sons!

At the end of the month we were told to meet in the canteen and as we assembled, our immediate future was uppermost in our minds. We were asked if we had any preference for which colliery we were going to be sent to and of course the northerners were all right, as they knew of places near to their homes. But us southerners did not stand a chance. I had never given coal mines a thought up until now. Most of us said that we'd like to go to Betteshanger in Kent to be near home, and it was the only pit we knew of, but nobody was posted there. It was not until I saw a programme on the television in the 80s that I learnt why they would not allow us to go there, but at the time we were never informed. The miners in Kent were a militant bunch, they had come over from South Wales in the 1926 strike and the last thing they wanted was to have disgruntled Bevin Boys there to be indoctrinated against things. So we were not allowed to go, and knowing how important coal was, you could see their point of view.

When I was asked where I would like to go I thought of Bransby Jones, the vicar of St. Andrew's, our parish church in Moulescoomb, and remembered what he had said about his last parish. It was a mining village in North Wales called Llay, and the colliery was Llay Main, so this is what I said, and they agreed to it. I had no idea where it was or how to pronounce it. I was told later by my landlady that I was the first 'Bevin Boy in North Wales,' not that it meant anything to me for I did not want to be a coal miner. I only wanted to be a sailor. Doug Langdell chose Jubilee Mine as it was near to his home.

A QUICK DASH HOME

Nearer the time of our departure we were given travel warrants to our collieries. To my knowledge the idea of choosing the colliery you wished to work at was soon abolished and you were told where you would be going. I feel sure that no places had been organised for us at that time. The authorities were still feeling their way at this stage.

We finished on the Friday when we had to pay up all the money for digs, but we were allowed to stay there until the Monday. This was when next month's call up would arrive. I hoped that they would fare better than we had.

The call of home was strong and it would be good to see Brighton and mum and dad again, if only for a short time. I could not wait to get started and made my plans. I would also get a chance to go and see Bransby Jones and tell him where I was off to.

I had enough money to get home, so I caught the train on Friday afternoon. I was sitting in the carriage, happy and anticipating seeing home again, when suddenly a mass of Royal Air Force lads got on; I had never seen so much stuff in my life. They had oranges, bananas and muscatels in diamond shaped packets. My eyes nearly popped out of my head at such a sight. They had just flown in from training in North America and were on leave. What is more, they had just received their wings and were very boisterous and happy with their lot. They asked me what I was doing there and after a short explanation we all tucked into the food and beer. It was like celebrating Christmas in February. This was the best train journey I had ever been on. As we neared

Euston Station the train stopped some way short of the platform, and we were there for half an hour or so. In the end one of the Air Force lads said, 'Come on, I can see the platform, we're not staying here all day.' So we opened the carriage door, dropped down onto the track and walked to the platform. There had been an air raid and the train had been kept outside the station. This was the first time that I had done anything like that in my life but I did not think twice about it and just followed.

I arrived home tired from a difficult journey because of the air raid. Mum and dad did not know that I was coming because we did not have a telephone. Come to think of it, I did not know anyone who did, well only the vicar. But if I was late there was always a key hanging on a piece of string just the other side of the letter box: I could still get into the house. At the first opportunity I went to see Bransby Jones to explain where I was off to. He gave me the address of Mr Haynes the local postmaster of Llay, and after a flying visit I returned to Coventry. It had been good to see Brighton again.

NEW HORIZONS

The place was deserted when I arrived back except for two or three of us southerners who were starting down the local pits. I collected my warrant to go on to Gresford. The name Gresford rang a bell with me, but I could not remember for what reason. I was to learn at a later date of the terrible pit disaster there in 1934, which I have never forgotten.

When I caught the train to Wrexham I had little spare money in my pocket and carried a pair of boots, a hat and a scrap of paper with a name written on it. I am sure Hitler must have been scared stiff of this very efficient force I was now part of. I did wonder at this moment, and many times later on, what I was doing for the war effort. Years later I would be told what a total waste of time and energy the whole Bevin Boy scheme was. I was here by the pick of a number so had to make the best of it.

I waited patiently on the station for the connecting train, which was to take me to Gresford. If I had only known I could have caught the bus for 4d and it would have taken me to Llay without any bother. Llay was the next village to Gresford but I did not know this at the time. The train was one that stopped at every station, and it puffed slowly along the track. I had plenty of time to think of home and the girl friends I had left behind. I was feeling slightly homesick for I had fallen in love for the very first time. Letters in the weeks to come would help me through this initial period for I felt so lonely in a land where many spoke a different language, and the pubs closed all day on a Sunday!

Leaving Gresford Station I started the walk into Llay very apprehensively. I had so little to carry, for my worldly possessions were few. I hoped I was walking in the right direction for the village. Ahead of me I could see a man fishing from a bridge over the River Dee and thought back to the days when the beach and piers in Brighton were places to fish from. All too soon the war had put a stop to that pursuit. I approached the man and asked him if I was on the correct road, pointing to the name written on the paper, for I felt awkward trying to pronounce the Welsh names. Wheezing, he said, 'Up the hill and round the corner, its not far.' His name was Tony Pant, a good sounding Welsh name – or so it seemed to me. When I worked with him some years later, I was to find out that this was his nickname.

When he gave me the directions, his breathing was very difficult and laboured. The cause was a mining accident. A joint blew on the main pipe taking compressed air to the whole of the mine. When it blew, it forced a lot of stones on to his back, injuring him permanently. He was given a lighter job in the pit as were other injured workers, and believe me there were many. On the positive side they were always retained if they could still work, if only to do cleaning work in the locker and shower area. Another thing I was to find out very soon was that coughing and spitting to clear your lungs was part of daily life in the mine. The same as the Welsh habit of adding the job you did to your surname. I was to become Les Bevin, who everybody knew because I was the only Bevin Boy in the pit.

MR AND MRS LEWIS

I was still looking for the Post Office and Haynes-the-Post for I needed a bed for the night, so I left Tony Pant to his fishing and continued towards Llay and the colliery. Before long I found the Post Office and Mr Haynes inside it. I handed him the envelope with the note in it written on the back of a St. Andrews' magazine and signed by Bransby Jones. I am sure that if I had not been feeling so apprehensive I would have enjoyed the situation. Here I was, out of the blue, one pair of boots, a hat, white shirts and a pair of trousers with a stripe down the side, ready to save old England (and Wales). I did hope the army, navy and air force were better organised.

The postmaster did not know me from Adam. Nothing had been organised and no one had been informed of which day or month I was to arrive. No digs were arranged. I had little money with me, so could not put up at a hotel or anywhere else, and here I was with one scrap of paper by way of introduction. I just hoped Adolf Hitler did not know how the country, and in particular the Bevin Boy scheme, was being run. I have since wondered what would have happened if I had just disappeared into the countryside. I am sure no one but my family would have noticed.

I knew Haynes-the-Post had been the church warden at the time when Bransby Jones was the vicar of Llay, and I was completely at his mercy. Nobody could have chosen a better person to help me. Mr Haynes gave me a meal and went to visit someone he knew to see if he could fix me up with some digs. I was told that we would know in the morning if he had been successful; the reason being that the lady's husband was on shift, and she felt that she must ask him first before taking in a lodger.

I slept the night in the Post Office. The morning arrived and the answer that Mr and Mrs Lewis of 43 Seventh Avenue, Llay, would take me in. A few years ago I learnt what went on when Teddy (I never called him that) Lewis returned from the pit. Mrs Lewis explained the situation and asked for his opinion on what she should do. He said, 'The answer is all very simple. If you had a son (they had one daughter, Alma) and he was in Brighton, what would you want Mrs

Wilson to do for him? Now you have the answer.' So this was how I came to be their adopted son. I think that some higher authority was looking after me.

Mr and Mrs Lewis and Alma, Rhyl 1945

The first thing I did was to explain my position to them both. I could not give them any rent immediately, for the colliery kept one week's wages until you had finished working for them. This meant that I must work two weeks before getting any pay. I was told not to worry, we can work things out together: and we did.

Mr Lewis said that he would get some information for me when he went to work that day: 'I will tell them you are here with me.' At that moment I felt sure that even the colliery had no idea that I was to start work there. When Mr Lewis returned I was told that I was on the same shift as him in the morning. 'Don't worry,' he said, 'I'll see you are alright.'

The next day at a quarter to five in the morning (what a time!) I got up and dressed ready for work. I had to be there at six. I did leave the white collar and stud off the shirt; it somehow did not seem appropriate. Mr Lewis had got up before me and cooked breakfast for us both. He eyed me up and down with a wry smile and mentioned that he would see Mrs Lewis about some other shirts. 'I haven't any money to pay for them,' I said, feeling embarrassed. 'We will sort something, stop worrying,' he replied.

INTRODUCTION TO LLAY MINE

It was nearly a mile walking to the pithead and we were not alone. Many others were walking as well, for all the houses around were owned by Llay Main Colliery and occupied by mine workers and their families. Other people were ferried in by bus from the surrounding districts, as there was something like two-and-a-half thousand workers at the colliery. The massive waste tip dominated and scarred the skyline. Many years later it was cleared and used to make the M6 motorway.

On arrival at the pithead Mr Lewis took me to the washroom and secured a locker next to his. He also got me a towel, which you had to buy. The soap was given to you but rationed to one bar a week. You were issued coupons for this, so could not exceed the ration. I still had not earned a penny and still had to pay for all this. I could see that at this rate I would end up in prison - debtors' prison! I was given two locks, one for the clean locker and another for the dirty locker. The showers were large enough for three people to shower comfortably. I put my soap and towel in the clean locker. The number on both lockers was 1190, this was also my lamp check and wages number. When you collected your lamp, you left a disc with your number in its place. By the time all of this was completed Mr Lewis had to go and start work and I went to meet Ernie Garston, who was to train me in my new occupation. I bet I stood out like a sore thumb the way I was dressed.

Meeting new people and learning all about the different trades proved very bewildering at first. There are two main types of people in the mine, haulage and colliers, the colliers being the more experienced. Mr Lewis was a collier. There were also electricians, railmen, ropemen and many others. They all had their own place to make the mine run smoothly. Some worked above ground, others below, and of course there was the office staff. Unlike most offices some of these were located at the bottom of the shaft. Maybe with my white shirts I would secure an office job, but no such luck came my way.

Being from the south and the first Bevin Boy they ever had, I was to be shown around the mine and got to see areas out of bounds to many. They were proud of their place of work and of being a miner. 'We go down at 8 o'clock,' Mr Garston informed me, and a strange feeling rippled through my body as I had learnt that the shaft was about half-a-mile deep. News travels fast around the grapevine of the mine.

Most of the face workers had started their shift and when we arrived at the pithead ready for the descent into the bowels of the earth, Mr Garston and I were the only two going down. Many others were ready to go but were holding back. In no way were they going down with us. I wondered why as I heard them saying, 'We are not going down with him, for all the tea in China.' The fear within me increased. They all knew what I was in for.

Mr Garston and I entered the cage. The safety gates were closed and we were off for the drop of a lifetime. The man in charge of winding men up and down was the most skilled person I came to know. He could put the cage down on a wine glass without breaking it. At this time I had little knowledge of his great skill. Today, his great joy was to try and bring my breakfast back. I did not know at the time that there is a safety trip arrangement, which is engaged when winding men. This cuts in if the cage travels too fast. My initiation ceremony was to begin, I was going to say in DEAD EARNEST but it was no laughing matter at the time. The whole thing took off and gathered speed, banging and bumping. Would the bottom ever arrive? Or would we arrive too soon? Would it stop in time? Would my breakfast remain just a memory, or return as a second helping? The drop seemed endless. I wondered when the man winding the cage would know when we had arrived, but he was an artist and a perfectionist in his job. We slowed and halted at the bottom in one piece. The cage was in just the right position to step out in comfort, and to my relief, breakfast remained a memory, but only just. I felt now that it was over, I was proud and a miner. Those we left at the top would have a much more comfortable trip a little later.

Situated at the bottom of the shaft were the offices with all the usual things that offices contain. For someone like me that had always worked in a shop, it seemed incredible that such places were so far below the surface. The mine manager and the undermanager were already at work in their respective offices. The one real difference was that these were held up with pit props – I found it unbelievable. I was taken into an office to see the mine manager Mr Holmes and then Mr Garston took me around and showed me the pit. At one point he stopped and said we have something here from Brighton, and there in front of me was a set of large switches with the name Allen West on them. I suddenly felt at home and wondered if dad had worked on these. I had often heard him say that they did work for the coal mines and that the switches had to be special so that any spark did not cause a fire. I think that these switches were known as 'flame proof.' I could not take in all the new things that were shown to me. I do wish that I could recall my feelings at this time. The brain was suddenly flooded with so much information in a very short time that only a small amount remains. We went up a little roadway in the bowels of the earth, and at the end of this a group of men were opening up a new coal face. I was told that I would start work with these lads. 'They'll show you what to do.'

Stan, Michael and Les 1939

Mum and Dad 1960s

Sainsbury's, 55 London Road,
scene of the 'white feather'

Les and the Lewis family 1993
Back row: Alma nee Lewis, 1st left; Mrs Lewis, 4th left; Les's
wife, Marion, 4th right; Phyllis nee Lewis, 3rd right; Les
'Bevin', 1st right

MY FIRST DAY

I cannot recall how long this took, but by now the mine was in full swing. They had started to wind coal. This would mean that the cage was going at full speed. The mine once achieved seventy-six windings an hour, so you can guess how fast the cage was going up and down the shaft. I had noticed a draught on my back and queried this with Mr Garston. He seemed pleased with a question like this. 'You can always tell which way the exit is by that draught,' he said seriously. The need to find the way out in the event of the light failing was always on people's minds and this was the sort of information everyone needed to know. 'The reason is,' he continued, 'that there are two shafts, one the air goes down, and one the air comes up. The latter one has a series of doors to prevent a back flow, so the air only goes one way round the pit. Always face the draught to find the exit, son.' Fear rippled through me at the thought of being trapped down there and this piece of information remained with me always. Solidarity was important in all things especially where safety was concerned and the need to escape presented itself.

By this time it was snap time - yes SNAP, not snack. I was told that I would need a snap tin and a water bottle, I could easily drink three or four pints in a shift. I made a mental note: something else to buy. Snap lasted a quarter-of-an-hour. You had a cloth to dust off your hands, there was no chance of washing them and you would eat and drink where you were. I always took the *Brighton & Hove Gazette* down with me for something to read. Mum sent this paper regularly and it kept me in touch with home. When I had finished with them I would tuck them behind a roof prop, so one day if ever the mine is reopened, someone will find all these 1940s' papers, for I am sure they were never removed.

The inevitable question will be asked by many, as it always is, 'What did you do for the toilet?' The answer is simple, you dropped your trousers and sat on the side of a truck that carried coal. If snap time was called just after you had relieved yourself, you dusted off your hands and continued with your lunch. There were no toilets or facilities to wash your hands anyway. I do not remember ever hearing of masses of the work force going down with food poisoning. I am not saying that it was ideal, and there may have been significantly greater numbers suffering from stomach trouble than today, but that is all we had.

The tour over, I was allowed home after being told that I must join the union. This idea was foreign to me and I said quickly, 'I don't wish to join a union,' I had after all come from a staunch Conservative home: we had no time for unions. Someone in authority said, 'The whole pit will come to a standstill if you do not comply. No one will work with you.' I felt the pressure from the people around. 'What happens if you go on strike then,' I asked. 'You do know that I will be sent to prison don't you?' I was angry by this time. I did not want to come coal mining. I did not want to join a union. Oh this wonderful (free) country that most men were fighting for and I had wanted to be part of. The choice was very easy, for again, there was no choice at all.

The fresh air and daylight came as a welcome relief to the warm claustrophobic air of the pit. I did wonder how I would survive in the coming years, in these most unpleasant conditions. I had been used to the merry click of the bacon machine, and nice clean white shirts, starched collars and clean hands and nails. It certainly was 'a far cry from a white apron'. One day in the future the experience would be very frightening indeed, but for now I was on my way to Seventh Avenue and felt very proud of what I was doing for the country and the war effort.

SETTLING IN

In the morning I went with Mr Lewis to the pit feeling very much like the new boy. On arrival we took our outside clothes off and put them into the clean locker. There was heating running through them, so if you arrived wet, by the end of the day the clothes had dried off. It was fatal though, if you left your sandwiches in there by mistake. I changed into the odd assortment of clothes that mum had managed to get for me. Mrs Lewis had promised to get me some brown shirts when she next went into town. All the men wore brown shirts made out of coarse material, 'A couple will start you off,' she said, 'and don't start worrying about the money, we'll manage between us.' It was not only the money that worried me but I wondered if I had enough clothing coupons as well. The hat I was given proved to be too hot, and later I wore a woman's beret. They did not worry just as long as you wore a hat. Many men just had a flat cap, which was not how people envisage the typical coal miner - hard hat with a lamp fixed on it. A present day safety officer would have had a fit if he had seen us in those days. I went to work looking like a grocer and when I arrived at the bottom of the shaft I looked like an out-of-work French onion seller, minus the onions!

I worked for a couple of weeks with the same group of men. They taught me how to lash the empty and full coal trucks up. The man in charge was Johnnie Whitehead: White Head was his nickname. He was the engine driver and he controlled the rope that went right round the pit bottom. It was a colossal length and fed all areas around the pit. All these different trades and all the strange names made work rewarding, as I learnt all about being a coal miner. Most people were helpful, for they knew where I had come from and the route. Most of them were destined from birth to become a miner.

There were four coal seams: there was the Brassi seam and down below that, the Main. Then the Queen seam was underneath that and finally below all the others, was the Kennel. At this point you were some distance from the main shaft.

After a short time Ernie Garston decided that I was good enough to go into the workings. I was going to work on 14 face, a long face of 150 yards. I was told that I could go in with Mr Lewis. Working on 14 face meant that I would have to get in when the first rides went down at 5.30 a.m.

Each day was the same procedure: the walk to work, the change of clothing, the lamp collection and the long drop to the bottom of the shaft. We walked some 150 yards from the pit bottom and then got onto the 'man-haulers'. These were ordinary trucks with a large piece of wood across them supported by a centre bar. The ride was about three-quarters-of-a-mile. You just sat there with your light, snap tin and water bottle and rode this part of the journey. On the odd occasion someone in front would shout 'DUCK' and this message passed along the trucks very rapidly, as it meant that the roof had not been ripped down and headroom was very little. This was when a new area was being opened up. Again the need to help each other to avoid an accident was uppermost in every miner's mind. Stick together to stay alive.

We alighted (that sounds like the underground, so polite) and walked down some 200 to 250 steps from the Brassi seam to the one below. The steps were made of two spikes hammered in, with a block of wood across and then levelled off. You could only get one man up or down at a time, they were no wider than that. Some of the young lads could walk up the slopes on the sides. In that way you could pass people you met on the journey down. I was able to do that then because I was agile, but I could not do it now to save my life. At the bottom was another lot of man-haulers. We rode for about the same distance as before and then got out. During this part of the trip I asked Mr Lewis (he sat on the other side of the trolley to me), 'How much further to go then?' 'Oh,' he replied, 'you've got another 200 yards.' Since we were in the return airway you had to go through doors. There were four in all, two at one end and two at the other. You opened all the doors except the last one. You couldn't open that because the pressure was too great. You had to wait until you heard the first door go bang, then you could open the last door.

Before I started work I was taken by Mr Lewis to see the fireman, who was also the foreman and the safety officer. He checked for gas and saw that it was safe. It was very obvious to this man that I was a complete novice. 'Look you now,' he said, 'you've never been on this job before, so I will show you what's what.' I spent the whole day just wandering around level 14, like most new boys do on their first day at a new job, wondering if I would ever get the hang of things. I was taken up to the face where all the men, including Mr Lewis, were stripped to the waist, working extremely hard. They used to move eight tons a shift in very unpleasant conditions.

MAKING FRIENDS

On this tour of the face I was to meet someone who was to become a lifelong friend, Wilson Lloyd (even the names are back to front up here I thought). I was to learn later that he had voluntarily joined the mines. His job before this was in the forestry, and he lived at Penmachno near Betws-y-Coed.

Wilson Lloyd

He was a local, relatively speaking, and he also spoke Welsh. This advantage always played a part. He told me his job was driving an engine on face 14 and asked what I was doing. I explained that this was my first day on this particular job and was being shown around the face. I may only have been the Bevin Boy but we were destined to become firm friends, I had a great need for someone of my own age to get me through the early days. What better person than a Welshman, who spoke Welsh (in fact his English was very poor at the time). The Welsh speaking people in the pit were the minority though, so I had very little trouble.

FINDING MY FEET

My first proper job when I returned to the level on my next shift was to uncouple the wagons, which came in threes, and let them go to the loading end of the belt. This was a very easy job, except that you were on the receiving end of all the dust and filth that the pans produced when they were shaking the coal down onto the belt. It was known that I was the new boy and no one wanted this job – that's why I got it. I would leave work as black as the ace of spades. There were no masks provided and I would leave the mine with ears literally filled with dust, a nose that when you blew it you had enough coal for a fire, and phlegm and mucus so thick with coal dust that you could never see any white in it. I tried chewing tobacco like many of the others but hated it. Spitting was soon to become commonplace, even with me for this was the only way to get rid of some of it during the shift. I wondered what the insides of long-term miners were like. I have since wondered if you needed any fuel at a miner's cremation with the amount of coal dust that must have settled in their lungs, and now in mine. But still people were saying, 'bloody miners', at any hint of a strike to improve conditions. I was finding this out first hand, and my Conservative views were slowly being eroded, like my lungs probably were.

I stuck this job for about three months. In the end I kicked up a stink. 'Can't I have a change, can't someone else do this?' Well they were fair, and I must have served my initiation period like a model student, for I was put on 'roads' (so called just like above ground) for a period but I never got to drive the engine like Wilson Lloyd.

I moved around on level 14 until a vacancy came up on the top of 33's 'dip' (literally a dip in the road). I said I would have a go, just for a change. I was told it was the same shifts: in fact everything was the same, it was just that I went to the top of the hill, which meant that the journey was shorter by a mile from the last job I was on.

It was my job to lash empty wagons on to the 'rope' (a steel hawser). There was electric lighting on the top of 33 level and a massive electric engine. I marvelled at how the weight of full wagons was used to help pull the empty ones to save the strain on the engine. Most of all, it felt good to be away from the filth and excessive dust of the last job, but my thoughts were, 'someone else is doing it'.

I had a great time on 33's dip. There were four of us plus the engine driver, enough for a card school during breaks. One chap would cut our hair, which was quite a saving. This was a community where everyone helped everyone else, and with telephones everywhere we could all keep in contact with each other easily.

Every move made by the engine driver was controlled by bells: two rings for 'go,' one for 'stop,' followed by the number of rings corresponding with where we were working. The top of 33 was four rings, and the bottom of 33 was six. When the rope stopped, the driver would not continue until he had received the correct number of rings. This method of communication was so ingrained in me that even to this day when a clock strikes or I hear a series of rings, I translate this back into the mine code. If this happens in the middle of the night and I am awake, on odd occasions, I experience the weirdest sensation. Not only am I transported back in time, but also I can clearly smell the mine. Take a seed merchant's for example, they had their own distinctive smell when I was young. So had the coal mine. The fear that it held on occasions when a situation became tense and dangerous, it was then that you became fully aware of just how far under the earth you were. When others recall their wartime experiences, and have said that they are never truly free of some terrible episode in their lives, I do understand this. The fear and smell of the mine will be with me until the day I die.

The routine of work soon fell into a pattern, as did leisure time. I joined the local 'Boys' Club' with Wilson Lloyd. The cinema in Chester was also a frequent haunt for the pair of us, even though they had a cinema in the church hall at Llay. Travelling around the countryside in this part of Wales was not difficult, unlike what happened to me on my return to Brighton on leave.

CHANGING VIEWS

I had lost my identity card in 1943 and went into Brighton to renew it. This meant that the new one had a new number and was stamped the 21ˢᵗ June 1943. The old number I knew easily, EGCB 36/3. The new number YEGA 1251374 took me ages to learn. This card now contained my Welsh address 43, Seventh Avenue, Llay, Wrexham.

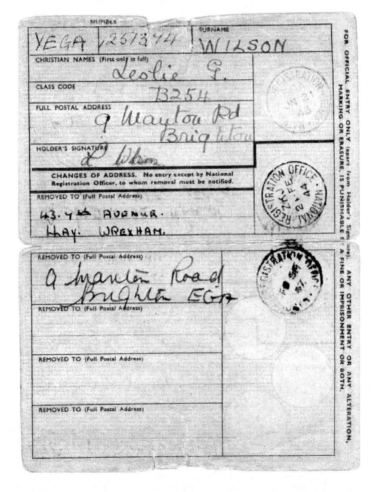

Brighton came into view and to me it smelt wonderful. Just the thought of being home was enough and I could not get there quickly enough. As I arrived at the barrier a policeman asked to see my identity card, which I duly produced. I took this as a matter of course until I was grilled for some moments on why, if I was a Brightonian, did I have a card with a Wrexham address on it? And what was I doing in civilian clothes? I could see it was going to be my luck that after getting so close to home I was going to end up in prison without a choice. I explained about being a Bevin Boy, which was to no avail. The identity card had nothing on it to say that I was a Bevin Boy. The policeman just did not want to know. Then at last, an old neighbour, who was a ticket collector at the station, came to my rescue. I pointed to Mr Lee and said, ' He will vouch for me.' Over he came and peered at me, and then at the policeman. 'Yes, he's OK, that's Les Wilson the Bevin Boy. He lives in Manton Road. I know him well.' Thank God for Mr Lee who saved the situation for me. For one horrible moment, I thought that maybe he would not recognise me and then I would have been sunk.

On this leave I was to understand the policeman's concern, for the town was packed to overflowing with troops and armaments. In areas where trees were leafy enough to conceal them, were large groups of tanks. I can only think this must have been the build up for D-Day. I felt sure that if any more had been packed into the south it would have tipped England up and everything would have slid into the sea. I also knew that I had to keep my mouth shut when I returned, 'the slip of a lip could sink a ship,' sort of thing. This would not be easy for me. I knew that people around Llay had no conception of what it was like in the south. The differences from Llay to here were so great.

Being home on leave was not easy, for I had changed. I had grown up and my whole outlook had expanded. I would stand up against my parents, who would quote what the papers said about the miners and on one occasion what had been written about a strike at Llay Main, which I was not involved in as I would have gone to prison. I recall that I spoke to the union leader and told him that if I were to go on strike and lose more than two days' work I must appear before the Pit Production Committee and explain why. I was told officially that I could not go to work by myself for safety reasons, and after all one Bevin Boy did not matter. The strike was over a coal allowance. They took five shillings a week out of your money for coal which was delivered to your house, a ton every five weeks I think; and if this lasted a year they still took five shillings each week. You were prohibited to sell the excess to anyone. It was not the best coal but was still a great deal if you could use it: which they knew you could not. Everything was done by coal: cooking, heating, even the fish and chips in the village were cooked by coal. The fire in the house was never out. Electricity was supplied by the pit for a set weekly charge, so the lights were never switched off either. The maximum electrical power would boil a kettle, and if you put too many lights on at the same time, the fuse blew. A lasting memory of 43, Seventh Avenue was that it was hot in winter, and bloody hot in the summer. The only difference was that the lights were turned off to reduce the heat in the summer.

My argument with my parents was simple. If dad's employers Allen West supplied something to dad that he could not use, and took money out of his wages each week to buy it, would he put up with it? The answer was, 'This is not what the papers say it's about!' Why are parents hidebound? I soon learnt that it was not only the film companies that distorted the truth.

I stood my ground. This was something that would never have happened before I left home. I was now a person with personal experience. I saw how miners were treated by mine owners. At one time these owners had been a virtual cartel, able to regulate wages and prices and therefore did not like the power of the union. I think my parents understood in a small way, but really needed the hands-on experiences to fully understand.

This strike ended after some heated arguments and some stone throwing. We were finally awarded an increase in wages. I think this brought the money up to £4.00 a week for haulage, which I took even though I did not officially go on strike. My sympathies were indeed very much with the men. Colliers were paid under a different system.

I must say though, these differences did not alter the love mum had for me and she still worried about the dangerous job I was doing. I suspect that she was very proud of me. When it was time to return to Llay I would be packed off with all she could spare, but I still felt that when they talked between themselves they said, 'typical miners', but I am sure this did not apply to me.

LIFE WITH THE LEWIS FAMILY

Some years later mum heard on the radio that there had been a pit accident at Llay. She took great courage (she hated using the phone) and used the telephone box at the bottom of Manton Road. She asked the operator for 'Trunks', (for you had to be routed and could not dial the number yourself) and finally got through to the pit. The person that answered was Percy Jenkins' daughter Iris. She said that all was fine and that she had seen me that day. The trouble was at Llay Hall, a small pit close by, not Llay Main Colliery. Now mum could sleep easily knowing that I was safe.

Mrs Lewis treated me like a son. I felt that at this time I became the son that she and Mr Lewis never had. I was taken to all the family gatherings and when their second daughter Phyllis was born, I was asked to be her godfather and accepted willingly.

There were areas in their family life that I did not venture into. This is the same in most families. Mr Lewis and I did have our ups and downs on occasions but never over money. I think that the first comment he made lasted for the whole time I was there, 'What would you want Mrs Wilson to do for our son, if he was in Brighton?' Ernest Bevin only provided me with heartaches. Mr and Mrs Lewis did their best to heal them.

Our one big difference was religion: they were Chapel and I was Church of England. I was unable to go to church very often because of working shifts. We had to work eleven shifts in two weeks, and this more often than not, meant Sunday. What I was initially unaware of was the distinction between the types of churches. Throughout Wales the division was the same. Owners and those in authority went to church, while workers went to chapel. The resentment was to pervade most of mining, whether slate, coal or copper throughout Wales and was the destruction of many communities. If you went to church and were not a person who attended chapel regularly, it was insinuated that you were on the side of the bosses in a dispute. The difference never came between us though.

A BRUSH WITH DEATH

Often when a weekend came I would be invited to assist some senior worker in the mine. These times could be the most rewarding and at the same time frightening. I was asked if I would like to go with the man who was shot firing. This was to be in my own time but counted as overtime. I thought it would be an experience and I was not wrong.

My job was very simple: I was told to stay at one point and not to let any person pass, even the mine manager. If need be, I had the right to hit him to stop him. Not that it would ever come to that, for he would understand the rules better than anyone. But the thought was nice! Maybe Ernest Bevin would try to pass me, but this was just wishful thinking. The fireman explained to me what he was going to do, and then he left.

I took up my position. I was now totally alone, miles underground with a fireman half a mile away who was going to let off explosives. It was a scary experience. I must surely have been a fool to volunteer on my day off when I could have gone to town instead. The extra money would come in handy though for the train fare home if nothing else, for I was only given one railway warrant a year to get back home and so needed this extra cash.

I stood for some time and started to hear my own heartbeat. The only other sound was the 'plucking' of the roof. This is caused by small pieces of the roof that break off due to the extreme pressure underground. I began to realise that the whole tunnel was on the move. I then turned off the light from my lamp and waited for my eyes to adjust to the dark. They did not, and of course would not. You could feel the dark it was so black. I began to understand the deprivation of solitary confinement and the fear of being trapped underground, waiting for help, which may never arrive, with the air getting rare. This thought flooded through my brain. I became acutely aware of my breathing and turned on the light very quickly.

It all happened very suddenly, the explosion, and the fireman's welcome return. 'Well done son, job over, thanks for your help.' He never knew what I had gone through being all alone. How over-imaginative my brain had become. The best part of it was that I got paid for the job and did not have to complete the shift.

On another occasion I went in to work on a Sunday to break through the Staffordshire fault. There is an underground fault which goes right through to Staffordshire. We were on this fault line when suddenly the coal seam changed its height and we needed to get back on it. This could change everything by a couple of hundred yards. I went in as haulage to help clear the waste. Most of the team knew of the dangers: it was very difficult. I was near a phone when it rang. The mine manager wanted to speak to the fireman. I went up to the face to get him and the fireman shouted, 'Get out! get out!' We climbed down the ladder very fast; it was only made from nailed struts of wood. It's amazing how quickly you move when the adrenaline flows. There was a huge bang and the whole lot came in. All the men got out. Machinery was lost in the fall, but no men. I was sweating that day. I stopped working for a bit on Sundays after that episode. The whole road had to be cut again - without me, may I say. I did not volunteer.

THE GRESFORD DISASTER

Once over this fault I went in again to earn some extra money (by now we were on the explosion coal). The older men started to talk about the Gresford disaster, Gresford being the next village to ours. I was told that you could smell the bodies of the men buried underground. I never could, but it did keep us on our toes.

The story went that many men had collected their pay and gone down the mine with it in their back pockets. There were a large number of men down the pit on that Friday night because a football match between two local teams was being played on the Saturday, which many men wanted to go to. They had worked double shifts to get this time off. The explosion and subsequent fire took the lives of 263 men in the early hours of Saturday 22nd September 1934, and of three rescuers later. Everyone in the area was very aware of this date, and the dangers of coal mining - most of all me.

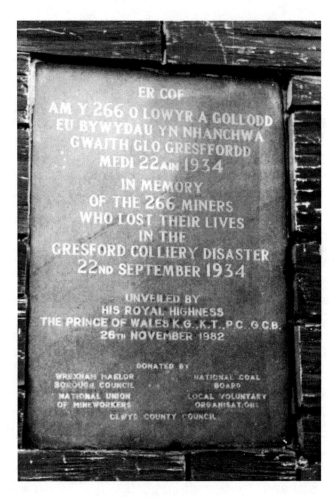

Gresford Memorial Tablet

I could see that people in the south of England could never fully understand mining, miners, miners' families and the structure of mining communities. If one person was touched by tragedy this radiated out, for it was so close knit. There was a need for unity to survive times like these. I became patently aware of this

Gresford Memorial

many years later when in 1966 I heard the news from a place called Aberfan where a slag heap slid down the hillside engulfing the village school, claiming 144 lives, 116 of which were children. I understood how the sorrow would affect the entire community.

The mine never went a long period without some injury to someone. You could stand waiting for the cage and out would come a stretcher with an injured person on it. One day it was a dead miner. The draught of the journey to the surface had blown the sheet from his face, and I would think there was a mother, wife or girlfriend somewhere to be informed of the loss. It was possible that the loss was made a little easier during the war because many others were receiving this sort of news of loved ones, but here in mining country this was ever present even before the war.

DIFFERENT TRADES

The different trades in the mine never ceased to amaze me. With the massive reduction in coal mines, I now wonder where all of these skills have vanished to. It was one man's job to check the ropes which lowered the cage that transported the men up and down. He would stand above the winding gear with a hand around the rope. The cage would be lowered slowly for him to assess the wear and tear on this important piece of equipment. When this was done the cage would come up and another checked. This sort of job was done at night.

When a new rope was needed to go round the pit (bearing in mind that it was a colossal length), it would be brought down and laid around the pit ready for the splicers to come in and complete the work. It meant that all the trucks had to be moved so that they could carry this out. Furthermore the working of the mine was not to be disrupted if at all possible.

The air flow down the mine was also constantly checked because if the fans stopped completely you had about twenty minutes to get out. The particular man who did this job had an instrument with a small fan in it. As this rotated it gave him a reading. He knew the safety levels very well and since he was already down the pit he would also be in trouble, as well as the other miners.

One day I asked if it was possible to go into the winding house but was told to ask again when I returned from my shift. I did so and this time they said yes. I felt elated because many long-term locals had never been allowed in there. My orders were not to speak to the man winding or distract his attention in any way. The size of the drum that the rope went round was enormous and it was tapered at both ends. There was also a dial with an arm that would tell the winder exactly where the cage was. A white line was painted on the drum and on the rope, and when these came together, the cage was at the bottom. The skill of the men who did this job was legendary. Each day you put your life in their hands and they honoured that trust put into them by others.

Electricians, railmen and an assortment of many other trades were ever present to keep the pit running smoothly, for we had a target to keep to with the amount of coal produced and anything to hinder this was reported to the production committee. I disrupted this flow one day.

REPRIMAND

The day started normally for me but the habit of working extra shifts so that I could leave early to catch a train home, became commonplace. On this day I may have become over confident; who knows?

I was working on the main rope at the pit bottom and I allowed a truck to go through with a chain still attached. The rope usually went through two star wheels, but on this occasion, because the chain was still attached, it came through, hit the star wheels and the whole lot flew into the air. The pit came to a total standstill and I was mortified. It was twenty minutes before it was all sorted out and production started up again.

I arrived at work early the next morning very apprehensively. I changed and went to pick up my lamp. A notice attached to it said that I must report to the manager at the bottom of the pit. All sorts of possibilities flashed through my mind but one thought was uppermost, they could not sack me. Mr Holmes raised his head and looked at me, 'What on earth happened yesterday then?' he asked. 'I don't know,' I replied, 'I must have been distracted for a moment. I am very sorry about it. I know it was my fault completely.' 'Well you know that I must report it, but don't let it worry you too much.' I almost let out a sigh of relief. He could not have been nicer about it. 'That's the first mistake I've made,' I said. His answer was brusque and dismissive. 'Right, get off to work, and be a little more careful in future.'

Whilst I was being given the dressing-down my eyes had wandered around the office and I noticed a map on the wall with a large cross on it. Ever inquisitive, I asked what this signified. Mr Holmes looked up surprised that I had not left. 'That's a map of the mine workings,' he replied. Still puzzled, I asked what the large cross on it represented.' That marks the spot where the church is situated on the surface,' he answered. A little mystified I asked why was it shown on this map, and his reply still baffles me now. 'Well we never take coal from beneath the church because it is consecrated ground.' With this I set off to work, wondering just how far you needed to go down for it to become unconsecrated ground.

I was moved soon afterwards to the bottom of the 'dip.' This was disappointing to me as I didn't get on with the people I was to work with. I had blotted my copybook and maybe it was thought that I was not able to do the last job and so had been moved to a less demanding one. I could see the reasoning but it was a pity, for I enjoyed the other place.

SICK LEAVE

On some of my days off I would stand where I could see the railway line and watch the Paddington bound train roar past. The steam and smoke belching out and billowing up as it thundered towards the south and home, felt in a strange way, romantic. I remained motionless, enveloped in the sooty air, until the train had vanished from sight. I am sure that inhaling this smoke did me little good but the mine with its dust must have been worse. Although the Lewis family were extremely good to me it was never home as Brighton was home, and to watch the train was a sure sign that I was homesick and that I needed to smell the sea again. I would do anything to get home. Working three consecutive shifts was always an option, because this gave me one extra day in Brighton. I never saw that fatigue could endanger myself or others. I was young and healthy and such ideas never occurred to me.

A visit to Doctor Henderson to have my ears syringed because of the amount of dust collected there, was just the start of my endeavours to try to get out on health grounds. I tried to say that the dust had caused havoc with my lungs as well; to no avail. Maybe too many other miners had tried this before me. The longest period of illness I had whilst mining was caused by an infection on the sole of my right foot. I had made an appointment to see Doctor Henderson because walking had become very difficult. On close examination he could see that the whole sole of the foot was going to come away. He started to pull the skin from the heel and removed a section that resembled the insole of a pair of shoes. His verdict was easy to arrive at. There was no way that I could work in this state. The possible cause was penetration of coal dust below the first layer of skin, causing infection and severe inflammation. He issued me with a sickness certificate knowing that I would be off work for some time.

I returned to 43, Seventh Avenue and explained my dilemma to Mrs Lewis. I would only be getting eighteen shillings a week sickness benefits, which would not even cover the rent and wondered if we could sort something out between us. She came up with the best solution of all. 'Why don't you get a holiday warrant and return to Brighton?' Which is just what I did. Mum looked after me for this period and of course there was no rent to pay. It took over a month for my feet to clear up before I could return to work. When I returned to Llay I had been moved from my last place of work - another change and different people to get to know.

The other time that I was really ill I was already at home on leave and had caught the 'flu. When the doctor came to see me I took the opportunity to ask him if I had stagmas (nystagmus). This was a complaint caused by continually looking at a small light source for prolonged periods. 'Why would you have that?' asked the doctor in surprise. 'Well I am a coal miner you know.' The doctor had not seen me for a long time and so he had forgotten. He assured me quite firmly that I had no such complaint. I tried everything I could think of but was never successful in getting a discharge on health grounds.

RELAXATION

When we worked day shifts together, Mr Lewis and I would get up at four forty-five in the morning. Mr Lewis cooked breakfast for us and Mrs Lewis had packed the snapping tins. This was four pieces of bread and a piece of cake each, or something similar. When we left the house in the winter, the change of temperature from the inside to the outside world was considerable. It was more noticeable because the houses were so warm with a constant fire burning day and night. On one occasion during the winter of 1946/47 we had to dig the snow away from the front of the house where it had drifted so high. We were unable to leave the house by the front door.

When I returned from the mine in the afternoons I was already clean, in fact I can never recall ever using the bath at No.43, for there was never any need to, it was all done at the mine. There was a bite to eat and then dinner in the evening. The Boys' Club in the evening was the main attraction, with the billiard tables being my highlight. We did have one rather lovely young woman who came to teach us ballroom dancing. For some reason she always chose me to be her partner. I never knew why at the time, because I had two left feet. How thick can you be? The only other reason I have since thought, could have been the fact that we both spoke the same language. What I mean by that is, she came from Croydon!

Also in the evening I had letters to write home. How I wish that we had the ease of telephoning, an action that we take for granted these days. The cinema (the 'flicks') and an insatiable appetite for reading supplied my every need for relaxation and entertainment, and of course the wireless. For me, the war was the wireless: Tommy Handley and ITMA, High Gang, Workers Playtime and the news. Whenever the opportunity presented itself, my ears were glued to it. My lasting memory of this time could only have happened in Wales: I sang in a choir and sang Messiah. To this present day I still have to join in when I listen to it at home. The words come flooding back. This was my whole life for the three and three-quarter years at Llay.

BRAVADO

At the same time there are incidents that I would prefer to forget. If I was to recall the one moment in this period that causes me more embarrassment now than it did at the time, it was this. Mr Lewis had taken me for a drink at a social evening in the Crown Inn, Llay, and the place was packed with Welshmen having a good time. Many people had done turns to a very appreciative audience. Suddenly the chairman turned to me and asked me if I would like to do anything. My reply was simple and enthusiastic, 'Yes, I would like to sing.' I stood up and the chairman hammered on the table shouting, 'Best of order please, singer on his feet.' The place went quiet and I started to sing the only song I knew all the way through. I shudder now at the thought of it. At the time I did not give it a second thought. Naivete and drink had given me Dutch courage. I burst forth into 'The Fishermen of England'. The applause was polite but certainly not rousing.

NEW CONCEPTIONS

The early months of 1947 were some of the coldest on record and with coal stocks very low, production at many factories ground to a halt. The other problem was the difficulty of digging the coal out from these stocks, for much of it was frozen. Eventually, I received an *Evening Argus* with a photograph of my father taken in Ann Street, Brighton on the 13th March 1947 queuing for coal. He was with four hundred others and the caption read: 'Picture taken today of part of a queue of four hundred people in Ann Street, Brighton. They queued from 8 o'clock this morning. Their reward – 28lbs of coal.' When I read this, I thought there must be a way to help them, for I was shifting tons of the stuff each day. I made my way to the mine manager with the paper and explained the situation. I asked if they would send down my coal allowance to Brighton to help my parents. He laughed at this request and told me that I must be joking. Well in a way I was, but it was worth a try. I could imagine mum and dad's faces if the ruse had worked out - but no such luck!

Whilst I was in Llay a vote was taken across Wales about whether to open the pubs on Sunday. The resounding verdict was NO. Llay was totally against it. So many of the locals, even those that had voted against the proposal, caught a bus and went to the first pub over the border for a drink on Sunday. I must say that I found this rather strange when many had such powerful objections to the proposal. I can only think that the attraction of the beer was greater than the conviction of the heart. On the plus side, this did make Sunday a very special day in this land of Wales. Another lesson had been learnt. What people say and what they do are two different things. As my father always said to me throughout his life, 'Actions speak louder than words.'

My time was fast coming to a close. My whole outlook was different; the change in me was to last forever but I did not know this. After the war many people were irrevocably changed by their wartime experiences. I thought my job at Sainsbury's would be waiting for me, but I knew for certain that I had thrown away the white apron forever, even at this early stage.

The one great difference that I understood but my parents and many others in the country never would, was that to mention Winston Churchill's name here in Llay when talking to miners, was like a red rag to a bull. The mention of his name was tantamount to blasphemy. The miners never forgave him for what he said during the 1926 strike, 'Shoot the miners, if they will not return to work.' People have long memories in a mining community and twenty years was but a short time. I had learnt about the conditions that people had been made to work under with little thought of their life and limb.

Whilst at Llay I was to see the change in the mine from a private to a nationalised industry. It was an interesting time for me, for I knew I would not be there forever so the effect would be minimal initially. At the beginning the effect was nothing at all, for almost everyone continued work as usual. All that really changed was the top person you were working for: it was now the Coal Board. The mine manager was the same, and each and every one did roughly the same work as before.

Standing on the sidelines, it was a joy to watch the way people reacted to the news of the changes. There were those that were close to the owners and their work prospects were linked in with them. They tried hard to disrupt the mine by telling the safety crews not to work and so bring the mine to a standstill. There was no great love between owners and miners. Most people had had a raw deal under them so when this idea was suggested it was turned down. No one was going to put their job in jeopardy. Many knew that they would not have any job at all if this happened. It made sense to change things from the inside, not from the dole queue. I think that the greatest change that each and everyone noticed was that old signs were painted out and new ones replaced them. For me it was the same old job, but one day soon I would be returning home and that could not come soon enough.

GOING HOME

The great day arrived when I was to leave. I received a letter to say that I could leave on Saturday 13th September 1947. This came two to three months before that date. I gave in my notice on Monday the 1st September. I was not expecting a leaving present but I did feel that some interest could have been shown. I explained to Mr and Mrs Lewis who were genuinely sad that I was going, but it did give them a little more room in the house. I had decided to leave for home on the Friday so I worked the extra time to enable me to do this.

On the day I gave in my notice, the mine suffered a 'gob' fire. The gob is the area behind the face that all the waste is packed into. Spontaneous combustion had caused this fire and the only way to extinguish it was to exclude the air. This means bricking the whole space up. All the trucks were moved out as fast as we could. As much equipment as possible was bundled along the mine to make way for the work. All the haulage workers on the dip were called in to do this work to bring the cement and blocks to the area. The fear got to me when the men came down with the breathing apparatus on and were carrying canaries. I had never seen this before. Someone had said the canaries had died and then compressed air was rushed down to force the gas out. The North Wales Mine Rescue team were also in attendance during this time, so it must have been very serious. I could see that in the event of an explosion I was going to end up dead, for I was right in line if this happened. Well, they did get it under control, but I thought that my time mining was not going to end on a happy note.

I finished the work on the Thursday, for I was on afternoons. I collected my pay and left my Brighton address so they could send on the week's money in hand that they still owed me. I went to the Labour Exchange for a railway warrant to get me home to Brighton, but my elation evaporated when an impersonal voice stated, 'You have had your holiday warrant for this year, you must pay your own fare home.' I was incensed at this and strove hard to keep my temper under control. I managed to say quite firmly, 'I was given a one-way ticket to Llay in 1944, I would now like the other half back to Brighton please. I will not leave this place until I get it.' Maybe some of my disregard for authority was the fact that I could not be sent to prison now. Finally the woman relented and produced a one-way ticket to Brighton.

Nobody said goodbye at the mine. I felt that after all my years spent there, someone could have said something, but I just disappeared. I packed up my few meagre belongings in a case, almost the same as when I arrived in 1944. These clothes were now brown shirts and trousers without a stripe down them. I kept my lamp check discs and one or two small items to remind me of my time at Llay Main Colliery, also most of my pay slips which I had retained for years, because I got fed up with the amount of people that hinted about the enormous pay packets I had received whilst mining. Then came the hard part: I said goodbye to all at No 43, Seventh Avenue, who had done so much for me in so many ways. The Lewis's were a second family to me and had done what they would have done for a son. They wished me well and a totally different person left, to the character that had arrived years before.

The change in me was marked, but more so in Teddy Lewis who had deteriorated in this short time from a fit collier, to a man who had difficulty climbing steps. He had been given a lighter job on haulage but finally had to retire from the mine for he had pneumoconiosis. His final days, some years later were I believe, spent gasping for breath in the Pantomime Ward in Wrexham Hospital. (A yearly pantomime was performed in Wrexham with the proceeds going to support this ward.)

I headed for the station and home to Brighton. I was walking on air now that I had the one-way ticket home. For me there was no demob suit and to kit me out to return to Sainsburys would take clothing coupons, which I could ill afford. I needed them for other articles in my wardrobe. I somehow knew that I would make good use of the brown shirts I had used in the mine. They certainly would not go to waste.

RECOLLECTIONS

I did not receive a hero's welcome on my return: neither did I want it. The war in Europe had been over for two years and four months. We were now looking towards the future. Mum and dad were pleased to see me back home again but it would not be easy for us all. I had left as an innocent youth but was now my own man. It was not so easy to have a Labour view in a staunch Conservative home and town, like Brighton. The challenge was good, for I had now got personal experience to show me the way.

Even though I thought my job with Sainsbury's was open to me on my return, I knew that I could not do this type of work ever again. I understand how, when people in the armed forces returned, their lives were irrevocably changed because of the war. This happened to me. I would never, and could never vote Conservative. My thoughts and aims were for the working man. When Winston Churchill regained the position of Prime Minister in 1951, I knew what the comments of the majority of miners of Llay Main Colliery would be, and sympathised with them.

The hunt for work soon began, because I needed to support myself in life. I looked at many options but thought all the time that I wanted a secure job for life. When one was offered to me I took it with open arms.

I joined the Southdown Bus Company working in the body shop, and this was to be my home until retirement. I was first at Victoria Road Portslade, but for the latter part of my working life at the Vicarage Garage in Freshfield Road, Brighton. Many people said to me when I had secured this, 'You now have a safe job for life, this is a wonderful company to work for.' The latter part of this statement was the only part to be correct. I finished my time with the company as T.G.W. Union, Shop Steward. I left the Southdown with stronger Labour views than ever. This was because of the way that the excess pension fund was misdirected, when Mrs Thatcher's government privatised the bus companies. Again all the workers lost out. In December 1985 she summed it all up and I quote: 'Of course there might have to be some losers.' You will note it is never Them.

During my stay in Llay, other men were to come to the mine, but there was never to my knowledge another Bevin Boy selected by ballot. These additional workers were people that did not wish to enter the armed forces. Some were conscientious objectors. Over a period of time, people eventually forgot how and when I had arrived at Llay. I had a distinctive southern accent, but so did many of the newcomers as well. I was soon classed with them by many of the miners, and this really hurt me. I felt that I wanted to shout out, 'I am not like them!' This was not a way out for me – I was forced by the government to come here. I am not a skiver trying to evade the army, neither am I a conscientious objector. I am a Bevin Boy. More often than not I found out later what was being said – and even that was second-hand. There seemed little use explaining. I knew the truth, but it still hurt. It still does to this present day. Little is ever shown on television about us. We have never been allowed to attend the British Legion Festival of Remembrance at the Albert Hall, and further more on Remembrance Sunday we have not been allowed to parade as an official body of miners at the cenotaph. There was some reluctant, small reference about us at the memorial parade on the 50th commemoration service to mark the end of the war. It is now fifty years since I stopped mining for this country. I really did think that I was doing my bit, and providing an important service for the country, by digging coal to keep homes and factories supplied with fuel. So did my parents, and I'm sure that Mr and Mrs Lewis and many other young lads forced into it felt the same. We were conscripts.

I had been told that there was a possibility of inclusion in the Remembrance Day parade in 1998. It would not matter if they had, for it is like saying to a dying man that you are sorry. Yes it helps, but the pressure to get it was hard and it is much too late. It matters little to many old Bevin Boys for they are dead, and I'm sure that many feel as I do now. We did as we were told, and we did our best for this country. Acknowledgement for what we achieved against the odds, would have been nice.

All these years I have never had the opportunity to be proud of what I did. I kept quiet about my time during the war, especially when this topic arose in conversation. It all started with that undeserved white feather, and ended with the student telling me, 'You weren't in the war.' I do not blame that student, for he was only telling me what others felt, but had not always had the courage to say.

My final thought on coal mining and politicians was when they closed Point of Ayr Colliery in North Wales in 1983. They questioned the relevant minister on television and asked him what he thought about closing Point of Ayr. His reply was, something like, 'It's a sad day for SCOTLAND.' That is how much they know or care. The common man means little to them. For most of them, it's just a well-paid job.

I have arrived at this stage in my life when it is reflective. I do not want anyone to go to war again. The experience for us all that returned is of a very exciting time doing things that we would never have done normally, but over these last years I have spoken to many people that have been emotionally scarred because of this period of their life. On this I can only repeat something I heard on television when men returned from the beaches of Normandy, that they'd fought on fifty years previously. One reporter told an old veteran, that the horror stories had so affected some reporters and cameramen that they needed counselling. To which he replied, 'You should have been here the first time.'

MICHAEL'S EPILOGUE

LLAY MAIN COLLIERY closed in 1966 and an industrial estate stands where the mine once stood. Where the colliery entrance was, a coal truck welded to some rails is all that is left to remind us of a once great industry.

In 1998 Bevin Boys were allowed to parade and march past the Cenotaph as an official body for the first time since the end of the Second World War. This has come about 51 years since Leslie stopped coal mining for this country as a conscript. However, they are still not allowed to participate in the Festival of Remembrance at the Albert Hall.

LESLIE'S EPILOGUE

AT LAST the pension money misdirected from the sell-off of the bus company has been fought for and reclaimed. I have been informed that my pension will be increased some time during the year 2000.

I last visited Mrs Lewis in a nursing home some months before she died but was unable to attend her funeral because I was recovering from a heart attack. I still keep in contact with both of her daughters Alma and Phyllis, and also Wilson Lloyd. I am always made welcome whenever I return to Wales.

ABOUT THIS BOOK

THIS BOOK was made by Janet Gregory, Jools Poore, Sheena Macdonald and Michael and Kathleen Wilson, with help from Andrew Breary, Steve Hill, Jack Latimer and Erica Smith. Thanks, too, to Jackie Blackwell and Jane Reid of QueenSpark for their support.

QueenSpark acknowledges help from J Sainsbury's archives, especially Adele Bland, for supplying cover photographs and picture of the interior of 55, London Road and to Hawarden Flintshire County Records Office for cover photo of Llay Main Colliery.

Sincere thanks to Dame Vera Lynn who, despite an accident, devoted time to writing the foreword to this book.

Printed by Digaprint Ltd, Hollingdean Road, Brighton.

ABOUT QUEENSPARK BOOKS

QUEENSPARK is a community writing and publishing group based in Brighton & Hove. We believe that everyone has a history and that anyone who wants to can be a writer. Our aim is to encourage and publish writing by people who do not normally get into print. QueenSpark Books is not a commercial company. We have two part-time paid workers, but the rest of us are volunteers. One of our aims is to produce books, gaining and sharing skills and confidence as we go.

We have several active writing workshops in Brighton and Hove. Our manuscripts group reads manuscripts that are sent to us and sets up book-making groups for those we are able to publish. All groups work on a co-operative basis.

QueenSpark Books is a member of the national Federation of Worker Writers and Community Publishers. We can give you the addresses of the other Federation groups.

QueenSpark gratefully acknowledges the support of South East Arts, the local council of Brighton and Hove, and the Foundation for Sports and the Arts.

If you would like more information, or would like to get involved in any of our activities, please contact:

QueenSpark Books
49 Grand Parade
Brighton BN2 2QA
Telephone and Fax: 01273 571710
Email: info@queensparkbooks.org.uk
Website: http://www.queensparkbooks.org.uk